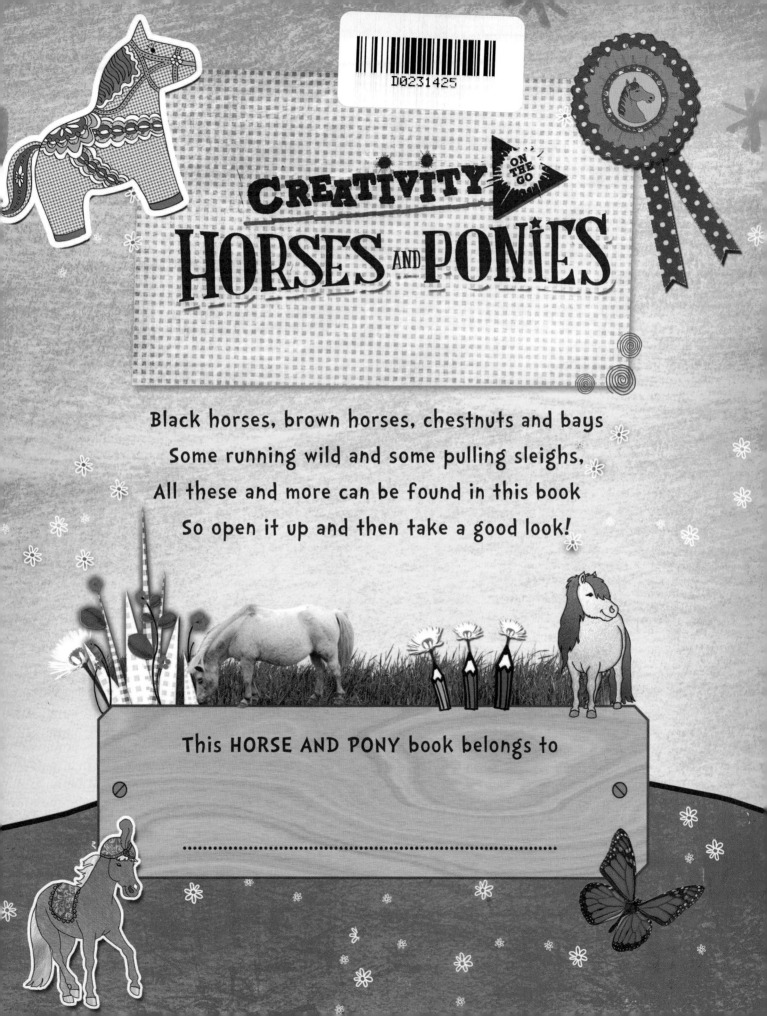

CREATIVITY
ON THE GO
HORSES AND PONIES

Black horses, brown horses, chestnuts and bays
Some running wild and some pulling sleighs,
All these and more can be found in this book
So open it up and then take a good look!

This HORSE AND PONY book belongs to

....

What's Inside this Book?

Stencils

Look for the horse and pony stencils inside. Hint: go to the back of the book, then search for the pages where you can use them.

Stickers

You will find your horse and pony stickers at the back of the book. Use them on the sticker scenes, quiz pages and anywhere else you want to!

Stories and pictures

There are oodles of things for horse and pony lovers to write, draw and paint, so get going!

Puzzle fun

Join the dots, find your way through a maze, match up the pairs, and take the ultimate horse and pony test.

Things to make

Make some special rosettes on page 21, some yummy muffins on page 28, cut-out ponies on page 57, some horsey hangers on page 61 and a flicker book on page 67.

Games

Will your horse be the winner on page 40? Or maybe your tail will be the one that hits the donkey's bottom on page 71!

This is a Carlton book

Text, design and illustration copyright © Carlton Books Limited 2012
Published in 2016 by Carlton Books Limited
An imprint of the Carlton Publishing Group,
20 Mortimer Street, London, W1T 3JW

A catalogue record for this book is available from the British Library.

ISBN: 978-1-78312-210-3

Printed and bound in China

Author: Andrea Pinnington

Publisher: Sam Sweeney
Art editor: Emily Clarke
Design: Amy Cooper
Senior editor: Anna Bowles
Illustrations: Jennifer Miles
Production: Claire Halligan

This book was made by Andrea Pinnington for the girl who loves horses, Olivia Page.

Are you mad about horses and ponies? Would you do anything to have a horse or pony of your own? Is every spare moment of your day spent thinking about horsey things? Then this is the perfect book for you. Complete all the horse and pony activities and become an official horse and pony lover (see page 79).

The Wonderful World of HORSES and PONIES

Complete the horse and pony pictures below.

BLAZE, THE DASHING STALLION

Blaze is not an easy ride and never lets
it be forgotten who is in charge.

NIBBLES, THE NAUGHTY SHETLAND

Worryingly, this mischievous creature
is usually ridden by young children.

SHANDY, THE SHOWY SHOWJUMPER
Shandy is rather temperamental and can either jump
beautifully or not at all (here seen in not-at-all mode).

4

SANTANA, THE SLEIGH HORSE

Santana lives high up in the mountains and spends the day pulling a magical sleigh. Listen out for the jingling bells.

TWIGLET, THE FILM STAR

Glamorous Twiglet is a celebrity horse. Never happier than when she's being prepared for a day's filming.

DAVE, THE SHIRE HORSE

Big is beautiful is Dave's slogan. Not the brightest horse around but certainly the largest. Seen here with Nibbles.

PEBBLES, THE PERFECT PONY

Pebbles is every rider's dream pony. Unlike Nibbles, she never kicks, bites, shies or bucks.

How to Draw a Pony

Copy the picture into the empty frame opposite.

Try drawing one square at a time.

Down at the Stables

Draw a horse looking out from each stable door.
Don't forget to fill in their name plates as well.

Add some tasty treats for your horse to eat.

FACT:
Popular horse and pony names often come from colours and markings (Star, Blaze, Honey, Pepper), jewels (Ruby, Silver), posh people (Prince, Lady) or weather (Misty, Storm).

Horses aren't the only creatures you'll find in a stableyard! You could draw in a cat, a dog, or maybe some mice.

Amazing Things to do
with your Pretty Pony Paper

1 Turn the page to find some dazzling pony paper. Why not use some of it to cover a little notebook? Then keep a look out for horse and pony pictures in old magazines. Cut out the ones you like and stick them into your pony perfect notebook. Don't forget to make up names for them as well.

2 Use the pony paper to make your own pictures, cards or bookmarks. Grown-ups love hand-made presents like these.

3 Cut out the pony patterns that appear on the back of the paper and use them to decorate some of the Dala horses and ponies on page 16. That's another horsey job well done!

Always ask a grown up to help you cut things out.

Pony Patterns

Cut out these shapes and use them in this book or anywhere you like.

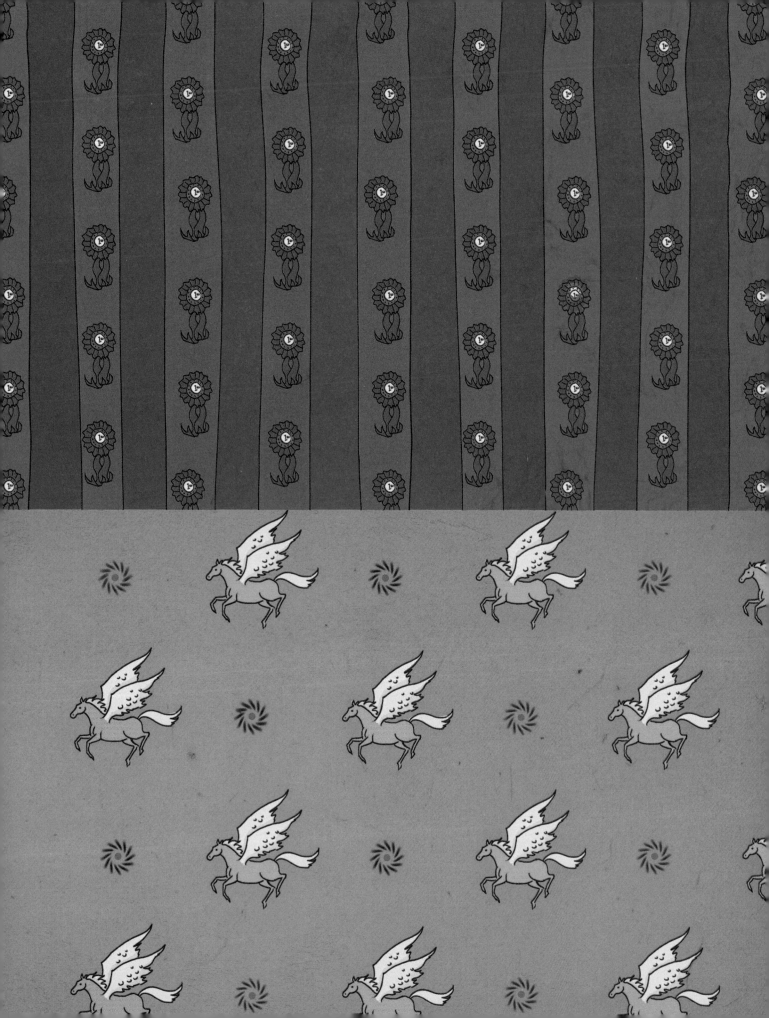

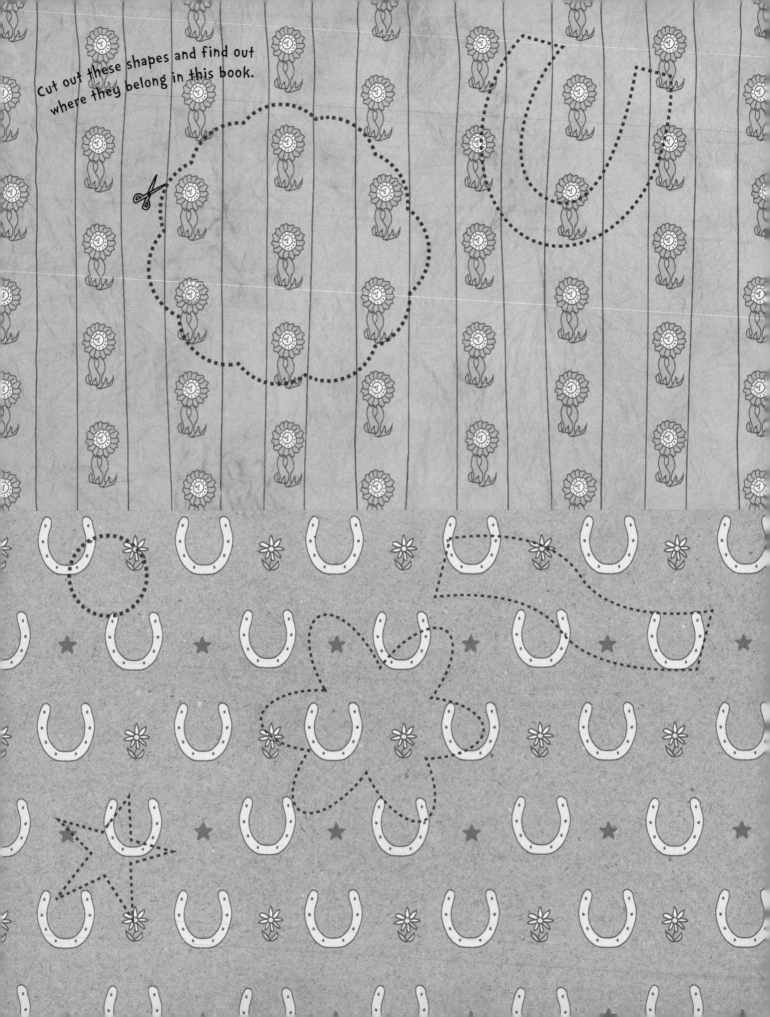

Cut out these shapes and find out where they belong in this book.

Showy Jumpers

Design and decorate your own magnificent show jumps.

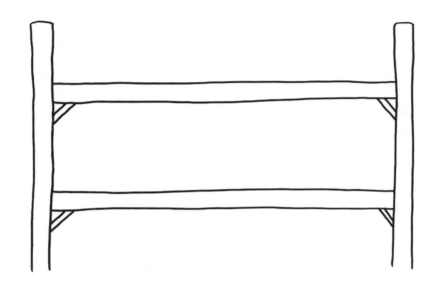

15

Dala Designs

Tucked away in small log cabins in the Swedish woods, parents used to carve wooden horses as toys for their children. These were called Dala horses. Colour in and decorate your very own Dala horses below. You can stick your horse paper onto them, too.

Spot the Difference

Yolanda the bay is rather pleased with her fancy new hairstyle and is showing it off to her friend Lady. Can you find eight differences between these two pictures, then colour them in?

FACT:
A person who looks after horses'
hooves and shoes is called a farrier.

Pony Express Maze

Can you help the pony express riders deliver all the mail? Make sure you pass the post to all the right riders as they make their way through the Wild Wild West.

FACT:
Pony express riders used to deliver the mail all across the USA. There would be teams of riders along the way as it was too far for one horse to travel.

The answers are on page 80

How to Make a Rosette

Why not organize your very own pony show and hand out rosettes like this one to the winners?

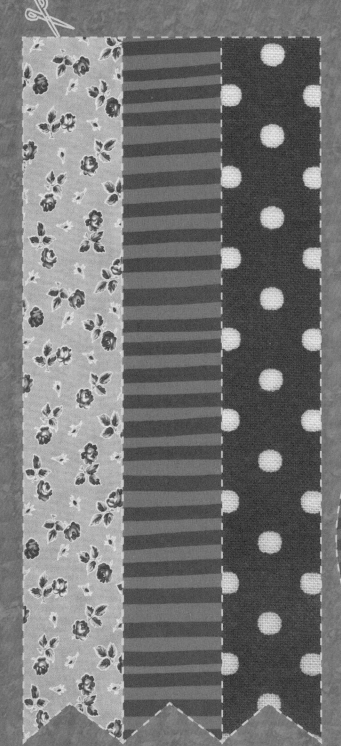

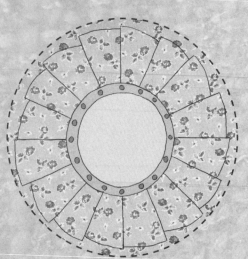

HOW TO MAKE A ROSETTE

1 Cut out the three rosette shapes: small, medium and large, then stick each one onto some card.

2 Now glue the medium rosette onto the centre of the larger one.

3 Stick the smallest rosette onto the medium one in the same way.

4 Finally, cut out the long strips of paper and glue them onto the back of the rosette so that they hang down like ribbons.

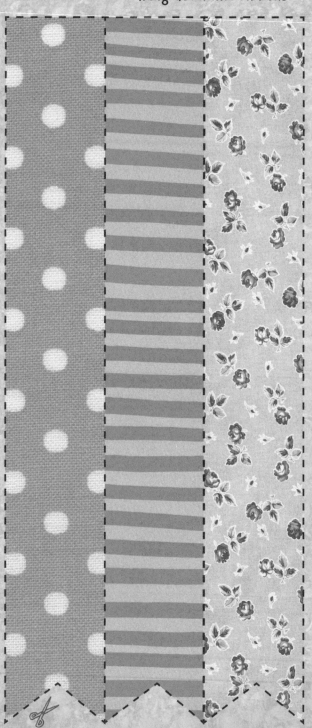

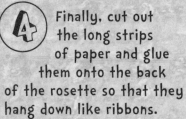

22

Once Upon a Pony Time

Complete the story shown in the pictures here.

Draw in the ending to your story.

. . . and he lived happily ever after (or did he . . . ?)

The Magical Unicorn Painting by Numbers

Complete the unicorn picture using the colour key below as your guide.

1 = purple   5 = dark green
2 = pink   6 = light blue
3 = black   7 = dark blue
4 = light green 8 = yellow

FACT:
A unicorn looks like a horse but has a spiral horn coming out of its forehead. Unicorns appear in lots of stories. They can often fly and have magical powers.

What Can You See?

How many riding hats, hoof picks and rosettes can you find in this picture?

FACT:
There is only one essential piece of kit to wear when you are riding and that is a hat!

The answers are on page 80

Horsey Who's Who

Read all about these famous horses and colour in their pictures.

BLACK BEAUTY
This is a book about a horse called Black Beauty and his two friends Ginger and Merrilegs. Black Beauty is sold to some terrible owners who mistreat him horribly, but he finally finds happiness.

THE WOODEN HORSE
Legend has it that there were once two warring armies: the Trojans and the Greeks. One day, the Greeks left a massive wooden horse outside the city of Troy. The Trojans dragged it inside the gates, little realizing there were warriors hidden inside. When night came, the soldiers escaped from the horse and took the city for the Greeks.

SHADOWFAX
In The Lord of the Rings, this beautiful horse is ridden by the white-haired magician, Gandalf. Shadowfax flies like the wind and has no need of a saddle or bridle. No one, save Gandalf, can ride him.

BLACK BESS
A long time ago, there was a highwayman called Dick Turpin. Riding his horse, Black Bess, he would stop coaches and ask the people inside to hand over their money. He was eventually caught and punished!

BUCEPHALUS
There was once a great leader called Alexander. When he was 12 years old, he tamed a wild horse called Bucephalus, who was afraid of his own shadow. He went on to ride this horse in many battles.

RED RUM
Red Rum was a real racehorse who won a famous race called the Grand National three times. This had NEVER been done before. He also came second twice as well!

How to Make Bran Muffins

Horses and ponies LOVE bran mashes.
Here's a recipe for some yummy bran food just for you!

You will need

- 100g (4 oz) butter
- 100g (4 oz) brown sugar
- 100ml (4fl oz) milk
- 3 bananas, mashed
- 1 tsp vanilla extract
- 2 free-range eggs
- 170g (6 oz) plain flour
- 100g (4 oz) wheat bran
- 1 tsp baking powder
- 1 tsp baking soda
- ¼ tsp salt

How to make the muffins

- Mix the butter and brown sugar together until light and fluffy.
- Then mix in the milk, bananas, vanilla and eggs.
- In a separate bowl, mix the flour, bran, baking powder, baking soda and salt.
- Then combine this with the butter and banana mix.
- Pour into some muffin cases and bake in a pre-heated oven at gas mark 4 or 180°C/350°F for 20 minutes.
- Place on a wire rack to cool.

Work Horses

Draw a line between the working horses and their matching owners.

Dot-to-dot Surprise

Join the dots to find out what sort of horse this is.

The answers are on page 80

Amazing Things to do with your Stencils

1 Turn to the back of this book to find your stencils. Use them to create your own horse and pony stationery like letters, birthday cards, invitations, notes and envelopes.

2 Decorate your bedroom by using your stencils to paint some horse and pony posters. Pin them up on your walls or door (first check that this is alright with a grown-up).

3 Use the stencils to make your own horse and pony notebook. Cut out and stick in any horse-related pictures you find.

4 Draw and write your own horse story using your stencils as inspiration.

The Jolly Jumpers

Use your stencils to draw some horses and riders leaping over these crazy jumps. Why not add some stickers too?

A Beginner's Guide to Horse and Pony people

There are lots of different types of people who love horses. These are some of the most interesting ones you may come across.

RODNEY THE NEW AND NERVOUS RIDER
Rodney took up riding at a late age. He's frightened of falling, being bitten or kicked, and generally of most things down at the stables. Many people wonder why he actually wants to ride at all.

SALLY THE SMART SHOWJUMPER
Sally always looks very smart. She spends ages getting ready before a show and other riders look on wistfully as she completes yet another perfect clear round.

JASON THE JOLLY JOCKEY
Jason was always the smallest boy in the class. He didn't like this very much until he discovered his talent for riding. He is now a world famous jockey where being small and light is VERY important.

CHARLENE THE RANCH HAND
Charlene is a ranch hand on a huge horse farm in the Australian outback. She can tame and ride any horse.

BABS THE HORSEY MOTHER
Babs is in charge of the local Pony Club. Her bark is definitely worse than her bite and she's the one to go to if you have a problem.

RODEO-RIDING RICK
Rick's been riding since he could walk, and he can keep his seat on a bucking bronco longer than anyone! Yee-haw!

A Pony of My Own

What would your perfect pony be like? Complete the pony pictures here by choosing some colours and markings for them from the boxes below.

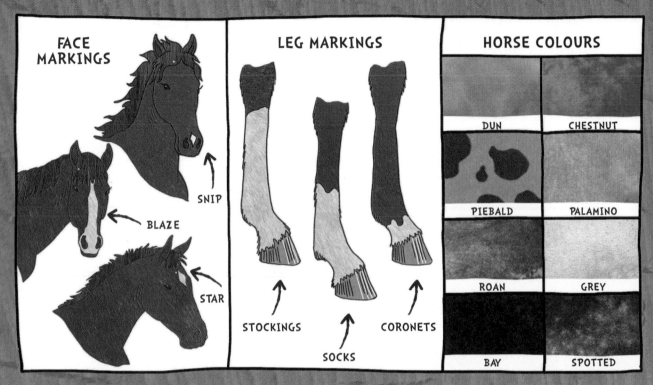

FACE MARKINGS

SNIP

BLAZE

STAR

LEG MARKINGS

STOCKINGS

SOCKS

CORONETS

HORSE COLOURS

DUN	CHESTNUT
PIEBALD	PALAMINO
ROAN	GREY
BAY	SPOTTED

FACT:
Horses have their own special colour
and marking names as shown here.

Racing Colours

Colour in and complete your own jockey cap and shirt designs.

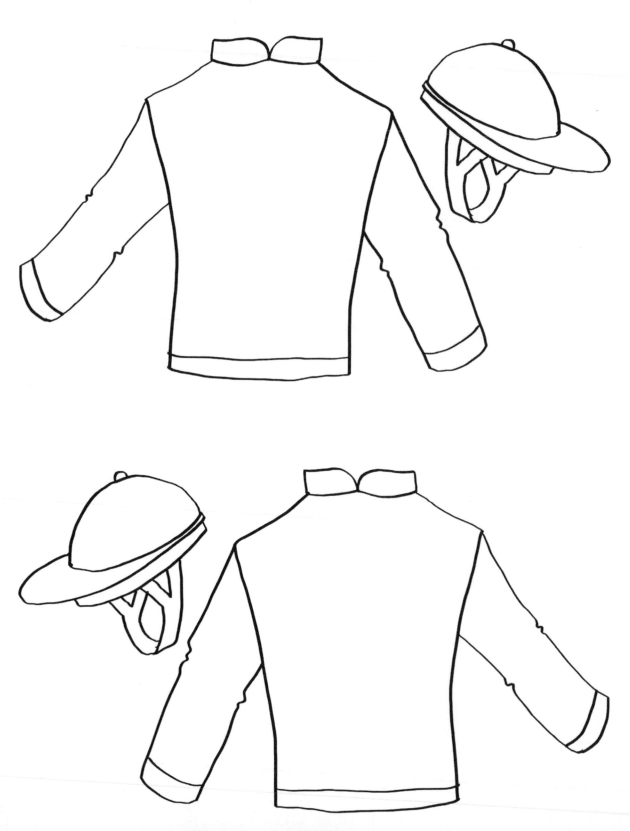

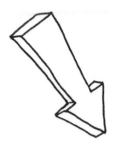

Now try making up something completely new.

FACT:
The colours worn by jockeys in races
are the colours of the owners or
trainers who employ them.

A Day at the Races

Choose a horse and watch it win, hopefully!
But look out, there may be some
unexpected obstacles
on the course.

HOW TO PLAY:

You will need a die and something you can use for horse counters (like buttons).

1 Place your counters on the START sign and take it in turns to roll the die. The first one to roll a six goes first.

2 Move forward the number of squares shown on the die and don't forget to follow the instructions on the course.

3 The first person to reach the FINISH LINE is the winner.

4 Take a turn in the WINNER'S ENCLOSURE!

1 Your horse forgets to set off with all the others. Miss a go.

16 Your horse begins to tire. Miss a go.

29 Your main rival retires hurt. Go forward one space.

12 One stirrup falls off. Go back two spaces to pick it up.

START

FINISH

WINNER

2 3 18 19 20 17 30 28 15 14 13

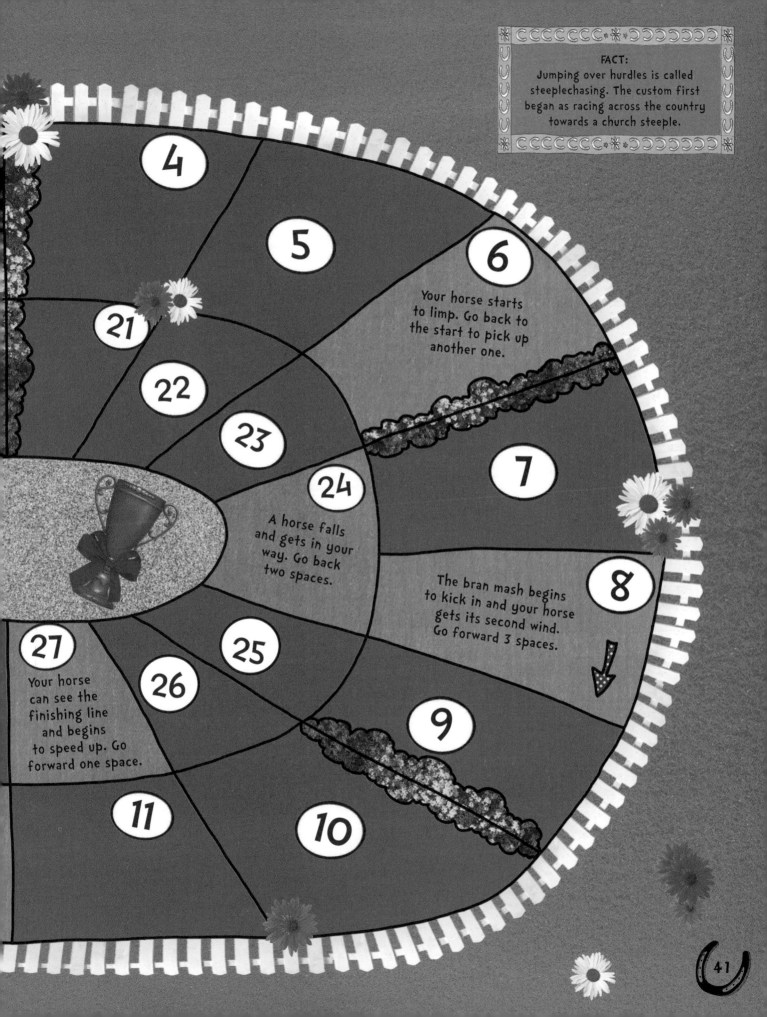

4

5

6

Your horse starts to limp. Go back to the start to pick up another one.

21

22

23

24

7

A horse falls and gets in your way. Go back two spaces.

The bran mash begins to kick in and your horse gets its second wind. Go forward 3 spaces.

8

27

Your horse can see the finishing line and begins to speed up. Go forward one space.

26

25

9

11

10

How to Draw a Cartoon Horse

Copy each step-by-step drawing into the boxes below.

Spot the Mice:
What's Going on at the Stable Yard?

Chaos has broken out in the stable yard!
How many mice can you spot in this picture?

FACT:
A groom is someone who is hired to look after horses or a stable. Not to be confused with the main man at a wedding.

The answers are on page 80

Magnificent Manes

Give these hip horses some wonderful
hairstyles down at the horsey hairdressers.

FACT:
Did you know
that horse
hair is used
for making
violin bows,
stuffing sofas
and for some
paintbrushes?

Pony Perfect: Test Yourself

How well do you know your horses and ponies? Find out by circling the right answers in this story.

One day, Jenny went down to the **STABLE/MANGER/GARAGE** to see her beautiful pony, Misty.

"Morning, Misty," she said, as she slipped on Misty's **ELECTRIC BLANKET/HEADCOLLAR/HARNESS**.

"We're going to a show, Misty, but first I need to clean out your **EARS/HOOVES/POCKETS**."

When Misty was shiny and clean, Jenny put on her **CLOTHES/HEADPHONES/TACK**.

Next she had to load Misty into the **TANKER/HORSEBOX/TRACTOR**.

Before they knew it, they were at the **HORSE FAIR/AMUSEMENT PARK/HORSE SHOW**.

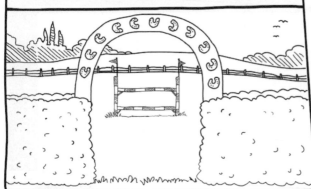

They jumped a **CLEAR ROUND/CLEAR COURSE/JOLLY JUMP** and won a **SPECIAL RED ROSETTE/FLOWER/ICE CREAM**.

46

The answers are on page 80

Pony Pairs

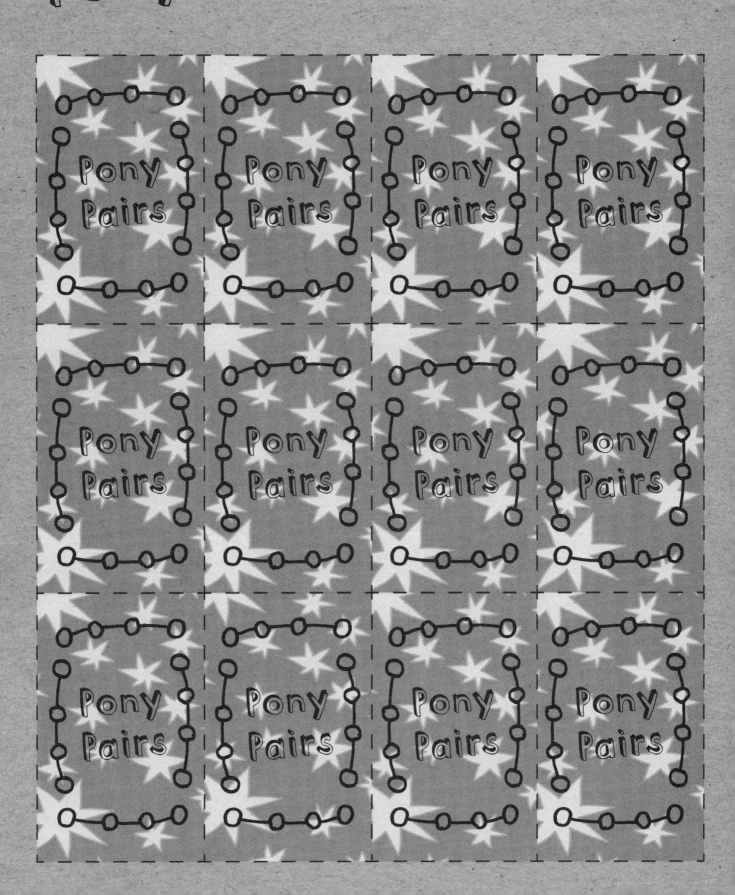

Pony Pairs

HOW TO PLAY:
- Shuffle the cards, then place them face down on a table or on the floor.
- The aim of the game is to try to find the most pairs.

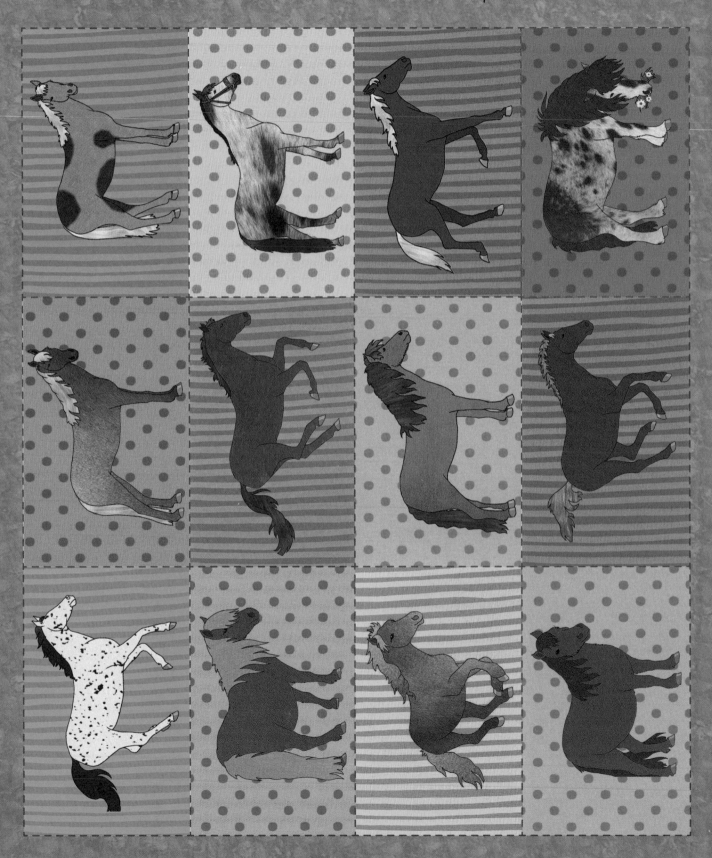

- Take it in turns to turn over two cards that you think might make a pair.
- If you find a pair, pick it up, then have another turn.
- The person with the most pairs is the winner!

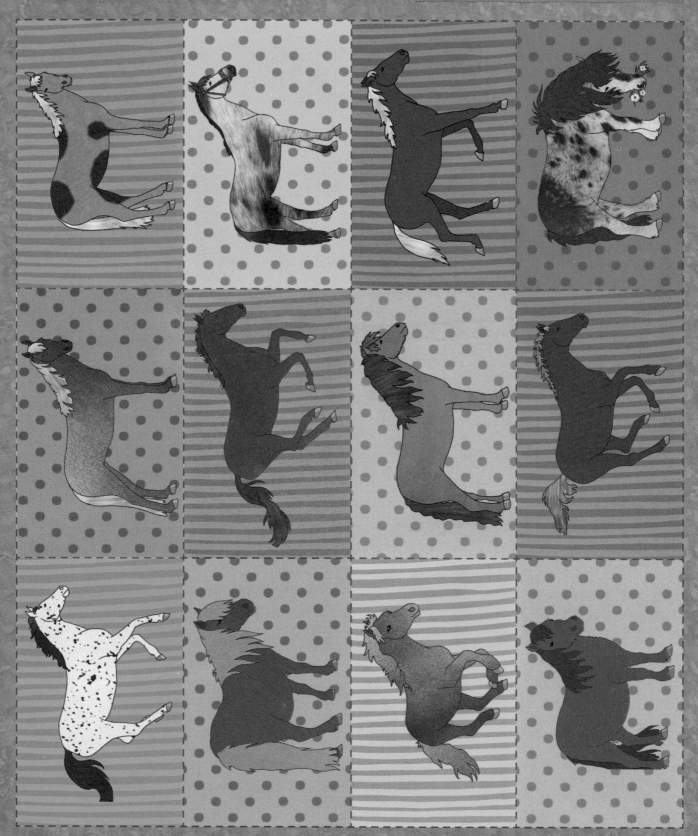

Pony Pairs

Cut out the pony cards, find a friend and get ready to play!

Perfect Pony Tales

Design a cover for this lovely book.

Don't forget to add an author!

The Story of Pegasus, the Winged Horse

Write the text to accompany a graphic retelling of this famous horse story. If you don't know it, it doesn't matter, you can just make up your own version.

1 _____
_____

2
_____
_____

3
_____
_____

4 _____
_____

5

_____

_____

6

_____

_____

7

_____

_____

8

_____

_____

Seeing Double

Can you spot two zebras that are exactly the same?

1

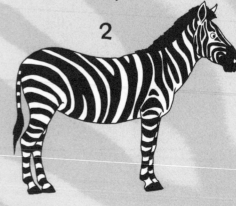

2

3

4

5

6

7

8

FACT:
In real life, no two zebras have the same markings. No one knows if they recognize each other by their stripes.

The answers are on page 80

SOS!

Sprite and Starlight have gone out for a canter and have got lost. Help them find their way home through the maze in time for supper.

START

FINISH

NOSEBAG

The answers are on page 80

Where Does it Go?

There is a whole set of special words used for talking about horses. Do you know your browband from your bit or your forelock from your fetlock? Choose the right words to go on the labels below.

MANE   HOOF
TAIL   FORELOCK
MUZZLE   STIRRUP
BROWBAND   GIRTH
BIT   NOSTRIL
SADDLE   FETLOCK

The answers are on page 80

Cut-out Ponies

Turn the page to find out what to do.

Fold here!

Fold here!

Fold here!

Fold here!

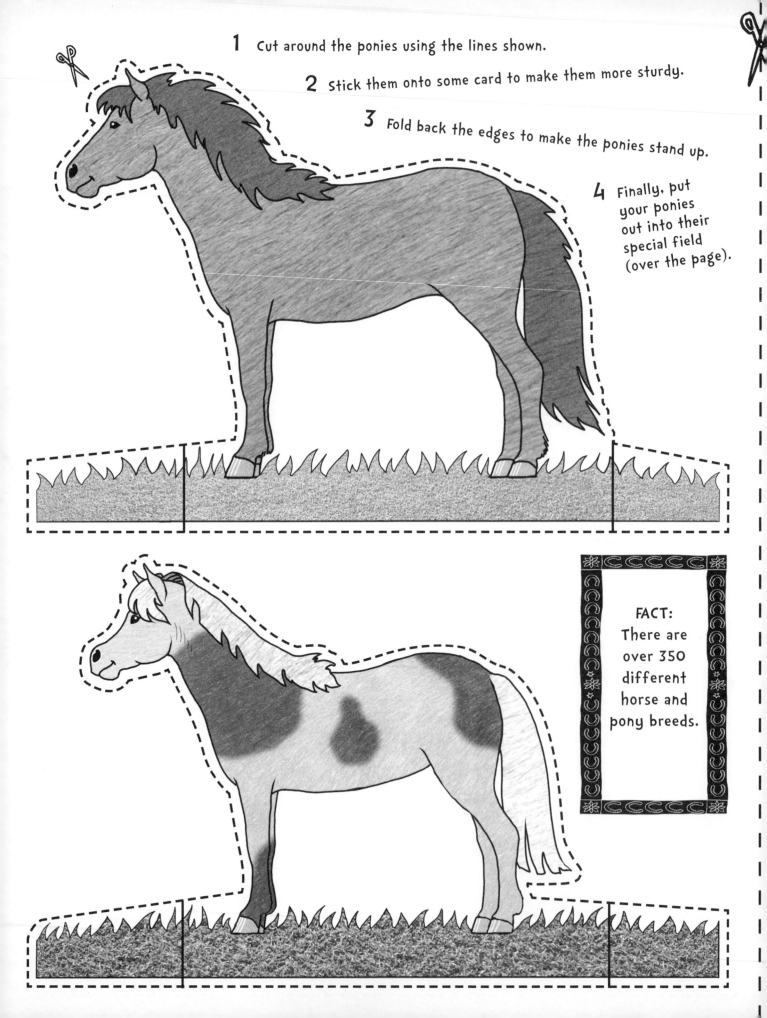

1 Cut around the ponies using the lines shown.

2 Stick them onto some card to make them more sturdy.

3 Fold back the edges to make the ponies stand up.

4 Finally, put your ponies out into their special field (over the page).

FACT: There are over 350 different horse and pony breeds.

Fields and Hedges

Once you've created your stand-up ponies
(see page 57), cut out this page and
use it as a base to stand them on.

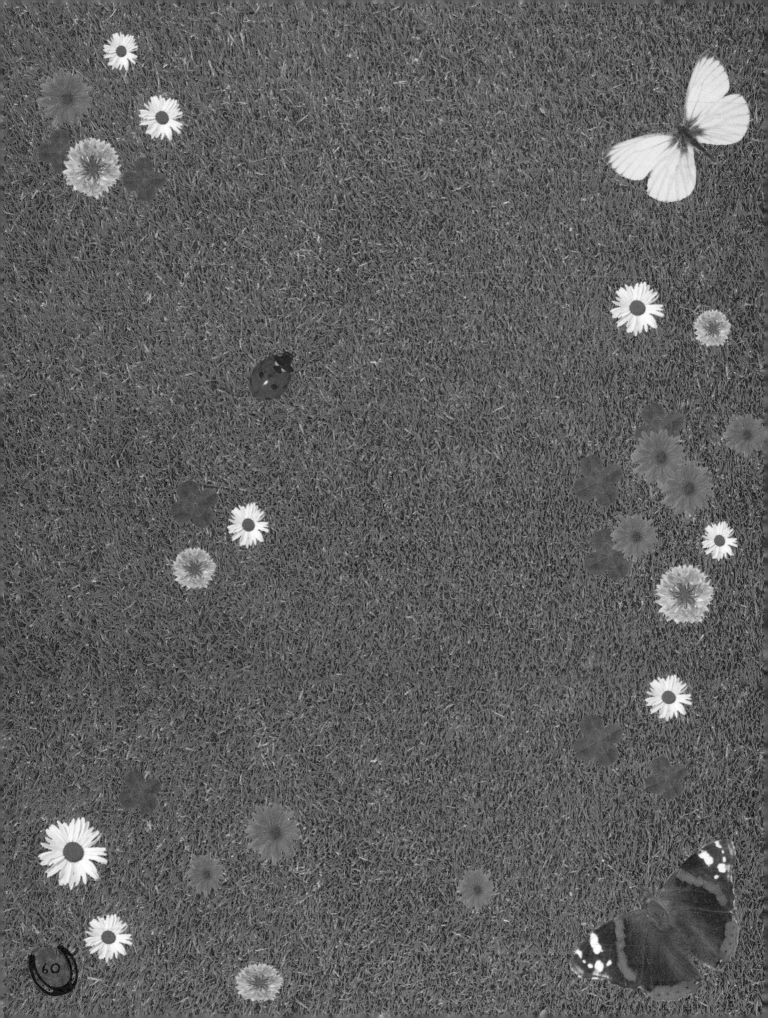

Horsey Hangers

Turn the page to find
out what to do next.

FACT:
Did you know that horses
sleep standing up?

Gone
for a
ride
back
soon

DO NOT
DISTURB
HORSE
NAPPING

Amazing Things to do with your Stickers

Take a look at the stickers on the special pages at the end of this book. You can play with them over and over again on the fold-out sticker scenes in the back cover.

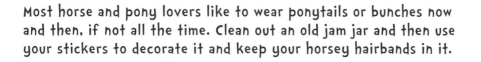

Look out for these other pages where you can use your stickers:

The Jolly Jumpers   (page 32)
Perfect Pony Tales (page 51)
Write your own Horse Story (page 52)
At the Horse Show (page 76)

Most horse and pony lovers like to wear ponytails or bunches now and then, if not all the time. Clean out an old jam jar and then use your stickers to decorate it and keep your horsey hairbands in it.

Ask a grown-up if they can help you create a small noticeboard, then decorate it with your special stickers. This is a great place to pin your rosettes, all your favourite pony pictures and any other certificates and pony papers you want to keep. Note: you can keep your Horse and Pony Lover's Certificate there, too (see page 79).

Horse and
Pony Lover

Certificate

Pony Camp Puzzle

Find the right stickers to complete this pony camp picture.

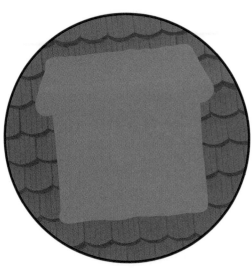

A place horses
call home.

You'll need to hold on tight
going over one of these.

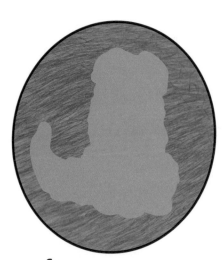

Someone else you
might find down at
the stable yard.

Sticker Quiz

Which stickers belong here?

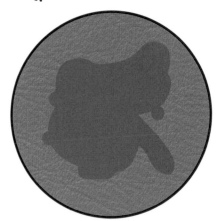

Something to sit on
when you go riding.

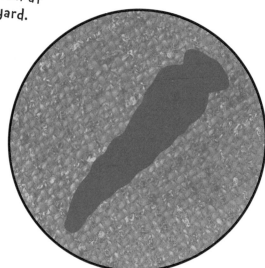

A favourite horsey treat.

You travel in a car.
A horse travels in
one of these.

Browbands and Body Brushes

Have fun colouring the horse and pony things below.

FACT:
Tack is the name given to the saddle, bridle and other equipment used on a horse or pony.

Flip Book Fun

Did you know that you can make a horse race or a donkey buck?

HOW TO MAKE YOUR FLIP BOOK

1 Cut out all the pages of the flip book.

2 Put the pages in the correct order, from the cover and page 1 through to page 27.

3 Ask a grown-up to help you staple the pages together.

4 Hold the book in your left hand, then flip the pages with your right thumb to watch the horse move!

My
Horse
Flip Book

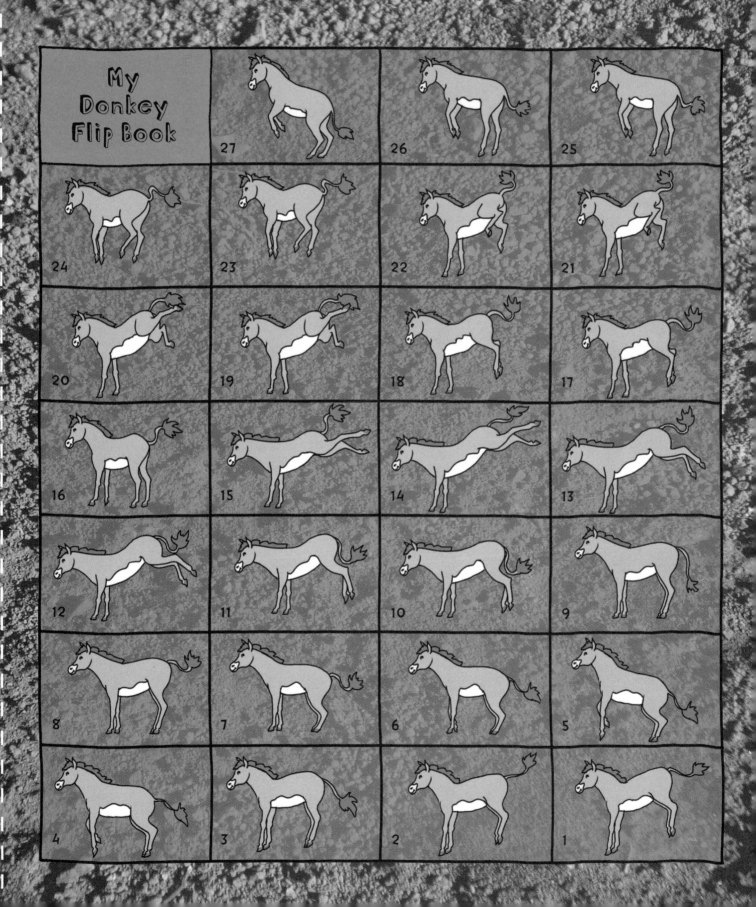

When you flip the pages of this book,
it'll look like the horse is moving!

HOW TO MAKE YOUR FLIP BOOK

1 Cut out all the pages of the flip book.

2 Put the pages in the correct order, from the cover and page 1 through to page 27.

3 Ask a grown-up to help you staple the pages together.

4 Hold the book in your left hand, then flip the pages with your right thumb to watch the donkey move!

Pin the Tail on the Donkey

Create your own version of this fun-filled traditional game!

1 Cut around the donkey and his tail using the lines shown.

2 Stick them both onto a piece of card and cut around them again.

3 Ask a grown-up to help you put a pin through the top of the donkey's tail.

4 Mark a cross on the donkey's bottom in exactly the place his tail should be. Now you're ready to play!

TO PLAY
THE GAME:

1 Take it in turns
to be blindfolded.

2 When you can't see,
try to pin the tail onto
the right part of the
donkey's bottom!

3 The person who
gets closest to the
spot is the winner.

Pony Postcards

Cut out and complete these cards and send them to your family or friends

What's wrong?

Can you spot 7 things that aren't right in this winter scene?

The answers are on page 80

At the Horse Show

Use your stencils, stickers and colouring
pencils to complete the scene.

add a trophy to the
winners' table

add a cat
chasing a
mouse

what is the weather like?

finish the bunting

add balloons here!

add a rider on this pony

Reasons Why I am a Horse and Pony Lover

I dream about
_____

I always
_____

I love
_____

I never
_____

I wear
_____

When I grow up, I would like
_____

Horse and Pony Lover

This special certificate is awarded to

....

for being a true horse and pony lover.

Signed by: *Pally Mino*

(Horse and Pony Lovers Club)

*If you're a horse lover,
loyal and true
The horses will know it,
and they'll love you too*

19

20

25

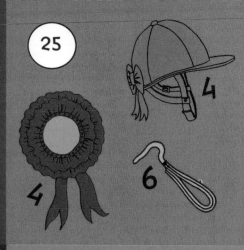

4

4

6

29

Answers

30

44

5 mice

46 Pony Perfect

❋ STABLE,
❋ HARNESS,
❋ HOOVES,
❋ TACK,
❋ HORSE BOX,
❋ HORSE SHOW,
❋ CLEAR ROUND,
❋ SPECIAL RED ROSETTE

54

Zebras
3 and 7

55

56

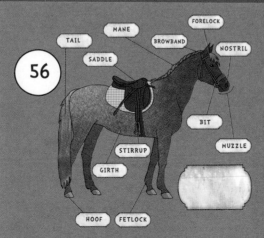

TAIL
MANE
FORELOCK
BROWBAND
NOSTRIL
SADDLE
BIT
MUZZLE
STIRRUP
GIRTH
HOOF FETLOCK

75